Dental English: Chairside Dialogues

Edited by Michio Tajima

Authors: C.S. Langham, Maiko Oshikawa, Michio Tajima, Tamotsu Uehara, Daniel J. Waldhoff

Lulu Press.com

Dental English: Chairside Dialogues

Edited by Michio Tajima

ISBN 978-1-105-52784-5

Lulu.com

Contents

Unit 1: At the beginning of the first visit

Receptionist: Good morning/afternoon/evening. (1   )

New Patient: Yes, I'd like to see the dentist about (2   ).

Receptionist: Is this your first visit?

New Patient: Yes.

Receptionist: (3   ).

New Patient: Sure, but I don't read Japanese.

Receptionist: (4   ).

New Patient: Thanks very much.

Receptionist: You're welcome. (5   ).

New Patient: Yes I do, here you are.

Receptionist: Thank you. (6   ). The dentist will be able to see you soon.

Translate the following Japanese sentences into English.

(1) どうされましたか?

(2) 歯の痛み

(3) この用紙に記入して下さい。

(4) 英語版もあります。

(5) 今日は保険証をお持ちですか?

(6) 記入し終わったら、返してください。

Unit 2: Asking about symptoms (1)

Dr. Ueda: Good afternoon. (1), please?

Mr. Jones: Oh, I'm Jack. Jack Jones.

Dr. Ueda: OK, Mr. Jones. This is your first visit. (2)

Mr. Jones: Tooth pain. Very bad. In the back of my mouth.

Dr. Ueda: OK, is it the right side or left side of your mouth?

Mr. Jones: Left.

Dr. Ueda: Is it (3)?

Mr. Jones: Yes.

Dr. Ueda: (4)

Mr. Jones: I think so, but I can't remember exactly. It's a long time ago.

Dr. Ueda: (5) since the treatment?

Mr. Jones: No, not really.

Dr. Ueda: OK. Do you feel pain when you eat or drink something hot or cold?

Mr. Jones: No, only when something gets caught between my teeth.

Dr. Ueda: Is it a sharp pain or just (6) or (7).

Mr. Jones: I would say, (6).

Translate the following Japanese sentences into English.

(1) お名前は？

(2) どうされましたか？

(3) 上の歯・下の歯

(4) 以前その歯を治療してもらったことがありますか？

(5) 何か痛みを感じたことはありますか？

(6) 不快感

(7) 少し刺激を感じる状態

Unit 3: Asking about medical history (2)

Dr. Ueda: (1) you feel any discomfort or irritation?

Mr. Jones: Do you mean other teeth? I don't know…

Dr. Ueda: I'd like to ask you about your health in general. (2), been in a hospital or had on operation?

Mr. Jones: No, never.

Dr. Ueda: That's great. Do you go to see a doctor?

Mr. Jones: No… well, I go to see a doctor for hay fever.

Dr. Ueda: OK. (3)

Mr. Jones: I take vitamin pills

Dr. Ueda: Do you know the name of them?

Mr. Jones: No, sorry, but I can check it and let you know the next time I'm here.

Dr. Ueda: Thank you. (4)?

Mr. Jones: No, I haven't.

Dr. Ueda: (5)

Mr. Jones: I don't think so.

Dr. Ueda: (6)

Mr. Jones: No, it's normal.

Dr. Ueda: OK, then, I'd just like to check your teeth. Please open wide.

Translate the following Japanese sentences into English.
The first two words are written for you.

(1) 他に何かありますか？

Is there

(2) 以前大きな病気をされたことがありますか？

Have you

(3) 何か薬やサプリメントを服用していますか？

Do you

(4) 麻酔の後に気分が悪くなったことがありますか？

Have you

(5) 薬や食べ物にアレルギーはありますか？

Are you

(5) 高血圧ですか？

Do you

Unit 4: Explaining treatment

Dr. Oshida: (1).

Mrs. Ogilvy: OK.

Dr. Oshida: You have two bad teeth in the back of your mouth.

Mrs. Ogilvy: I thought so.

Dr. Oshida: (2).

Mrs. Ogilvy: Will it hurt?

Dr. Oshida: You shouldn't feel much. I'll need to (3).

Mrs. Ogilvy: OK.

Dr. Oshida: Then, I'll put in a filling.

Mrs. Ogilvy: I see.

Dr. Oshida: Is there anything you want to ask?

Mrs. Ogilvy: No, not really.

Dr. Oshida: Thank you. I don't think you need anesthesia for the other bad tooth. But (4), too.

Mrs. Ogilvy: Yes.

Dr. Oshida: (5) from your teeth, while the anesthesia is good.

Mrs. Ogilvy: Thank you.

Dr. Oshida: Please (6). Now, please open your mouth.

Translate the following Japanese sentences into English.

(1) これから 治療について説明します。

(2) 麻酔をして、それから虫歯を削っていきます。

(3) 歯の神経を取ります。

(4) それも治療してしまいましょう。

(5) 歯石を取り除きます。

(6) 痛かったら左手をあげてください。

Unit 5: On a return visit for a checkup

Dr. Suzuki: Hello Mr. Aglio, how have you been? (1)

Mr. Aglio: No, I'm fine thanks, but I wanted to have you look at my teeth just to be sure (2)

Dr. Suzuki: Good. (3)

----- After checking -----

Dr. Suzuki: (4). But I suggest you have a thorough cleaning, though, (5)

Mr. Aglio: Thank you. I'll do that before I leave.

Dr. Suzuki: Good. When you are over 40, frequent cleaning can often prevent or lessen the likelihood of other illnesses.

Put the sentences a) ~ f) in the correct order to make a conversation. Then translate the conversation into Japanese.

(1.　　)
(2.　　)
(3.　　)
(4.　　)
(5.　　)

a) there is nothing to worry about.

b) Now the treatment is over.

c) Frequent checkups can prevent problems.

d) Is there any particular problem today?

e) I don't see anything to worry about.

f) we can make an appointment for you.

Unit 6: On a return visit for cleaning

Dr. Suzuki: Hello Mr. Aglio. How is everything today?

Mr. Aglio: Fine, thank you.

Dr. Suzuki: Good. We'll start the cleaning in a moment. (1)

Mr. Aglio: OK.

Dr. Suzuki: (2) .... now (3).

Mr. Aglio: Thank you.

Dr. Suzuki: (4). I'll cover your face with this towel. Is everything OK? Open wide.

Mr. Aglio: OK.

Dr. Suzuki: (5)

----- On checking for occlusion -----

Dr. Suzuki: Bite on this please. Now bite, bite, bite, and bite. That's good. (6) That's good.

Translate the following Japanese sentences into English.

1) 口をゆすいでください。

2) 前掛けをつけます。

3) 深く座ってリラックスしてください。

4) 背もたれを倒します。

5) 何か痛みを感じたら、左手を上げてください。

6) 顎を左右に動かしてください。右、左、右、左。

注：前掛けの他に、タオルやエプロンなども使うことがあります。

Unit 7: At the beginning of treatment

Dr. Suzuki: Good afternoon, Mr. Goodman. This is your first visit to us. (1) today?

Goodman: Well, I have had a pain in the back of my mouth.

Dr. Suzuki: Is that the right upper tooth?

Goodman: Yes, that's right. It started throbbing yesterday.

Dr. Suzuki: Hmmm, I wonder why. (2)

Goodman: I hope you can fix it today.

Dr. Suzuki: OK. (3)

Goodman: It's really painful. I couldn't sleep last night.

Dr. Suzuki: (4)

Goodman: aaaaggggggghhhhhhhhh.

Dr. Suzuki: You don't need to say anything right now, Mr. Goodman.

Goodman: oooooookkkkkkaaaay.

Dr. Suzuki: Now, I can see. (5)

Words to remember . . .

1) right upper tooth
2) throbbing pain
3) bad tooth
4) wisdom tooth

Put the sentences a) ~ e) in the correct order to make a conversation. Then translate them in Japanese.

(1.)

(2.)

(3.)

(4.)

(5.)

a) Head up, and open wide, please.

b) You have a bad wisdom tooth!

c) Let's have a look, shall we?

d) What seems to be the problem?

e) Could you open a little wider, please?

Different kinds of pain

1) acute pain
2) aching pain
3) dull pain
4) severe pain
5) sharp pain
6) throbbing pain

Which tooth

1) upper front tooth
2) lower back tooth
3) canine
4) wisdom tooth

Unit 8: An avulsed tooth/knocked-out tooth

Dental trauma / Dental injury / Dental emergency

Mr. Peebles's tooth was knocked out!!!

---1---

Receptionist: Dr. Aida, we have an emergency case.

Dr. Aida: What do you mean by "emergency"?

Receptionist: Well, a gentleman just came in and said that his tooth has been knocked out. He is bleeding.

Dr. Aida: I see, all right then, please bring him in right away.

---2---

A gentleman comes in:

Dr. Aida: Good afternoon. You are the first patient today.

Peebles: The first patient... but it's already 4pm.

Dr. Aida: I know... we don't have many patients these days... May I have your name?

Peebles: Peebles, Jonathan Peebles.

Dr. Aida: OK, Mr. Peebles. I'm Dr. Aida... So, your tooth has been knocked out, I heard.

Peebles: Yes, I was checking a travel guide, and suddenly bumped into a huge sumo wrestler.

Dr. Aida: A sumo wrestler...

Peebles: I fell on the ground and my front tooth was knocked out.

Dr. Aida: I can see you lost your upper front tooth...where is it now?

Peebles: I picked it up and have in my handkerchief.

Dr. Aida: OK, please let me see it.

---3---

Dr. Aida: It's not advisable to keep it in your handkerchief.

Peebles: What should I have done with it?

Dr. Aida: You should have tried to put it back in the socket yourself.

Peebles: Put it back! I don't think I could do that.

Dr. Aida: At least, you could have put it in saline solution or milk.

Peebles: But it just happened in front of your dental clinic a minute ago.

Dr. Aida: Is that so? You may be lucky.

Peebles: Lucky? Why?

Dr. Aida: If it's only a minute ago, we may be able to put it back in your socket. Let's see if we can save your tooth!

Peebles: Thank you.

Questions:

1. Why was Mr. Peebles's tooth knocked out?

   a) He ran into a sumo wrestler.

   b) He wanted to join a sumo club.

   c) A sumo wrestler attacked him.

   d) He admires sumo wrestlers.

2. Which tooth was knocked out?

   a) Maxillary central incisor

   b) Mandibular central incisor

   c) Upper third molar

   d) Upper canine

3. What is it that Mr. Peebles should not have done, according to Dr. Aida?

   a) Read a travel guide and walking at the same time

   b) Keep a knocked out tooth in a handkerchief

   c) Keep a knocked out tooth in a cup of milk

   d) Visit a dentist at 4 pm suddenly

4) Why did the dentist say Mr. Peebles may be lucky?

   a) Because he could hold his tooth in his handkerchief and take it home.

   b) Because the dentist may be able to put the tooth back.

   c) Because Mr. Peebles was the first patient and the dentist was not busy.

   d) Because only one tooth was knocked out, not several.

Key words

Informal English	Dental English
1) Knocked-out tooth	1) Avulsed tooth
2) Front tooth	2) Central incisor
3) Upper part of a tooth	3) Tooth crown

Phrases to remember

1) May I have your name?

2) Please let me see.

3) Put it back.

<Reading>

Dental Injury: what to do if a tooth is knocked out

1) Do not touch the root when you pick it up, but only the crown, the upper part of a tooth.
2) If the tooth is dirty, rinse it in a cup of water gently to remove the dirt.
3) Do not wipe it or hold it under running water.
4) Put it back in the socket if you can and bite down on gauze gently.
5) If the tooth cannot be put back, put it in saline solution or milk. Do not put it in tap water.
6) Seek dental care as soon as possible.

If the tooth was outside the socket for less than 20 minutes, the prognosis is better. All periodontal ligament cells die if the tooth is out of the socket longer than 60 minutes. It's important to get dental care before the root dries. Do not replace primary teeth, baby teeth, because loss of these teeth early does not hinder development of succedaneous teeth. If primary teeth are reimplanted, it may cause dentoalveolar ankylosis and facial deformities.

Immediate attention is a crucial part of saving an avulsed tooth. The longer you wait, the less chance there is for successful reimplantation.

Possible causes of avulsed teeth are

1) altercations/fighting
2) contact sports/ sports-related trauma
3) automobile/motorcycle/bicycle accidents
4) accidental falls
5) biting on hard food

After a major accident, your jaw may be broken if you are not able to open and close your mouth, or close your jaws properly. This requires immediate attention. You may call a dentist, but can also seek help at a hospital.

A long-term consequence can be shifting of the remaining teeth, resulting misalignment and periodontal disease.

Unit 9: Explaining medicine

Dentist: Please come again tomorrow. (1).

Patient: Thank you. I can come around 4pm.

Dentist: Great. (2)

Patient: OK.

Dentist: These are antibiotics. (3)

Patient: When should I take them?

Dentist: After meals for three days. And, these are painkillers. (4)

Patient: OK. I'll do that.

Dentist: (5)

Patient: Can I drink beer or wine?

Dentist: No, (6)

Patient: That's too bad. I should remember that.

Dentist: (7)

Key words

1) antibiotics: 抗生物質

2) painkillers: 痛み止め

Translate the following Japanese sentences into English.

(1) 歯を洗浄します。

(2) お薬の説明をします。

(3) 一日に三回、食後に一錠ずつ服用してください。

(4) 痛むときに、一錠服用してください。

(5) 何か質問はありますか？

(6) これらのお薬を服用する前後に、アルコール類は飲まないでください。

(7) お薬を飲んで気持ちが悪くなったら連絡して下さい。

Unit 10: Extraction

Pulling out a tooth

Goodman: Can you do something about this bad wisdom tooth? I couldn't sleep last night.

Dr. Suzuki: (1) and there is a lot of pus between the tooth and the gum.

Goodman: That sounds bad. Can you fix it today?

Dr. Suzuki: I'm afraid not. First, (2).

Goodman: What should I do?

Dr. Suzuki: (3) today.

Goodman: Will it sooth my swollen gums?

Dr. Suzuki: Yes, I hope so. I'll pull out the wisdom tooth (4).

Goodman: When will you do that?

Dr. Suzuki: (5)

Goodman: OK, if you say so.

Dr. Suzuki: I'll clean the tooth and gum for you now. (6)

Goodman: aagghhhhh.

Dr. Suzuki: You don't need to say anything, Mr. Goodman.

Translate the following Japanese sentences into English.

(1) 歯茎が腫れています。

(2) 歯についたよごれを取り除き、歯茎を清潔にします。

(3) 痛み止めと抗生物質を処方します。

(4) 炎症が引いた後に。

(5) 来週、親知らずを抜く予定をいれましょうか？

(6) もう一度、口を開けて下さい。

Answers

Unit 1

1. May I help you?
2. a toothache.
3. May I ask you to fill out this form please?
4. We have an English version.
5. Do you have a health insurance card today?
6. When you've filled it out, please return it to me.

Unit 2

1. Can I have your name
2. What seems to be the problem?
3. an upper tooth / a lower tooth
4. Have you ever had this tooth treated before?
5. Have you had any pain
6. discomfort
7. irritation

Unit 3

1. (Is there) anything else
2. (Have you) had any major diseases
3. (Do you) take any medicine or supplements?
4. (Have you) felt bad after anesthesia
5. (Are you) allergic to any medicine or food?
6. (Do you) have high blood pressure?

Unit 4

1. Let me explain the treatment.
2. I'll give you anesthesia, then, drill one of your bad teeth
3. take out some dental pulp
4. let's take care of it
5. I'll remove the tartar
6. raise your left hand, if you feel pain

Unit 5

1. d 2. a 3. c 4. e 5. f

Unit 6

1. Will you please rinse your mouth?
2. I'll put this bib on you.
3. sit back and relax please.
4. I'm going to lower the chair.
5. If you feel any pain, please raise your left hand.
6. Slide your jaw to the right, now left, right, left.

Unit 7

1. d 2. c 3. a 4. e 5. b

Unit 8

1. a 2. a 3. b 4. b

Unit 9

1. I will sterilize the wound.
2. Let me explain your medicine.
3. Take one tablet after meals three times a day.
4. Take one only when you have pain.
5. Do you have any questions?
6. do not drink any alcohol before or after you take these medicines.
7. Please contact us if you feel bad after taking the medicine.

Unit 10

1. The gum is swollen
2. I'll remove the food debris and wash the gum.
3. I'll prescribe some painkillers and antibiotics.
4. after the inflammation goes.
5. Let's pull out the wisdom tooth next week
6. Please open your mouth again.

メモ: 他にも覚えたい英語表現のリストを作りましょう。

1.

2.

3.

4.

5.

6.

7.

8.

9.

10.

メモ: 他にも覚えたい英語表現のリストを作りましょう。

11.

12.

13.

14.

15.

16.

17.

18.

19.

20.

www.ingramcontent.com/pod-product-compliance
Ingram Content Group UK Ltd.
Pitfield, Milton Keynes, MK11 3LW, UK
UKHW020228250726
13967UKWH00001B/252